Three
Dimensions

Three Dimensions

**MODERN & CONTEMPORARY APPROACHES
TO RELIEF AND SCULPTURE**

ACQUAVELLA

This publication accompanies the exhibition

Three Dimensions

**MODERN & CONTEMPORARY
APPROACHES TO RELIEF
AND SCULPTURE**

ON VIEW
September 25 – November 17, 2017

Acquavella Galleries
18 East Seventy-Ninth Street
New York, NY 10075

Library of Congress Control Number
2017953205

ISBN 978-0-9981156-2-7

DESIGN
HvADesign, NY

PRINT
Phoenix Lithographing, Philadelphia, PA

COVER
Pablo Picasso
Le Taureau (The Bull), c. 1949-50
Varnished wood and plaster
26 $^3/_4$ inches long (68 cm)
© 2017 Estate of Pablo Picasso /
Artists Rights Society (ARS), New York

FRONTISPIECE
David Hockney
Henry Reading, 1985 [DETAIL]
Collage, acrylic, contact paper, charcoal on
gatorboard in artist's frame
92 $^1/_2$ x 57 $^1/_2$ inches (234.9 x 146.1 cm)
© David Hockney

BACK COVER
El Anatsui
Metas III, 2014
Found aluminum and copper wire
110 x 114 inches (279.4 x 289.6 cm)
© El Anatsui

Plates

El Anatsui

PLATE 1

Metas III

2014
Found aluminum and copper wire
110 x 114 inches (279.4 x 289.6 cm)

Miquel Barceló

PLATE 2

Huîtres II (Oysters II)

1988
Mixed media on canvas
54 $^1/_2$ x 79 inches (138.4 x 200.7 cm)

Miquel Barceló

PLATE 3

Choux (Cabbage)

1996
Mixed media on canvas
78 $^3/_4$ x 78 $^3/_4$ inches (200 x 200 cm)

Miquel Barceló

PLATE 4

Peix de sorra (Sand Fish)

2014
Ceramic
20 x 12 x 10 $^{3}/_{8}$ inches (50.8 x 30.5 x 26.4 cm)

Louise Bourgeois

PLATE 5

Untitled

2002
Fabric and stainless steel
79 $^{1}/_{2}$ x 12 x 9 $^{7}/_{8}$ inches (201.9 x 30.5 x 25.1 cm)

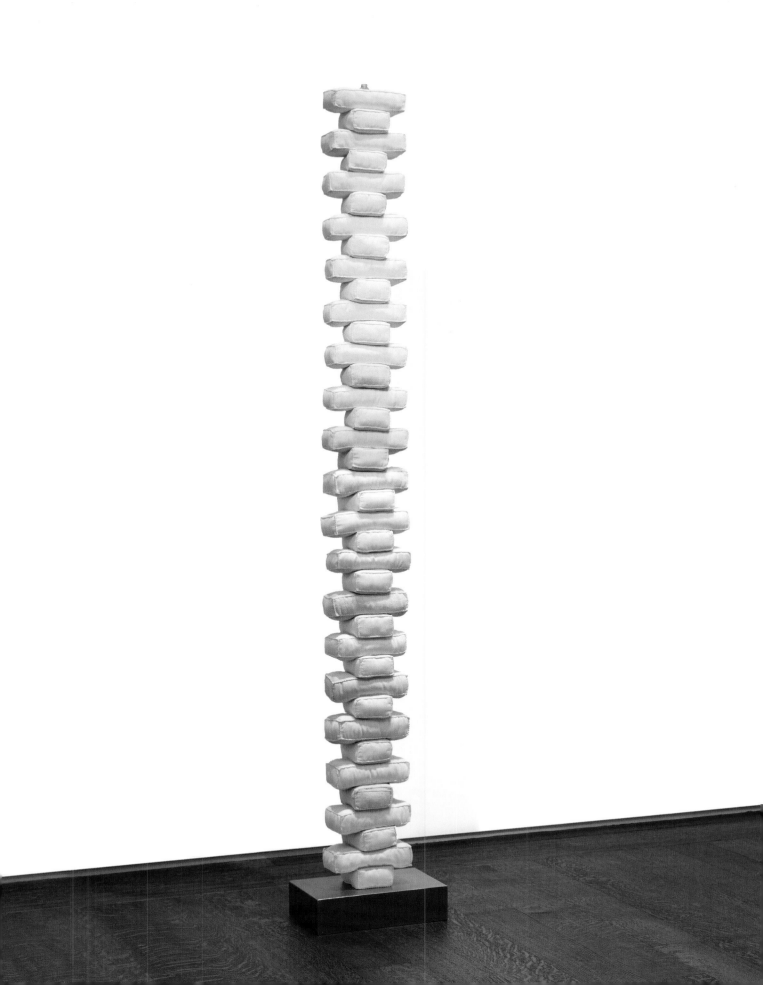

Alexander Calder

PLATE 6

Petits disques blancs (Small White Discs)

1953
Standing mobile: painted sheet metal and wire
33 x 38 x 27 inches (83.8 x 96.5 x 68.6 cm)

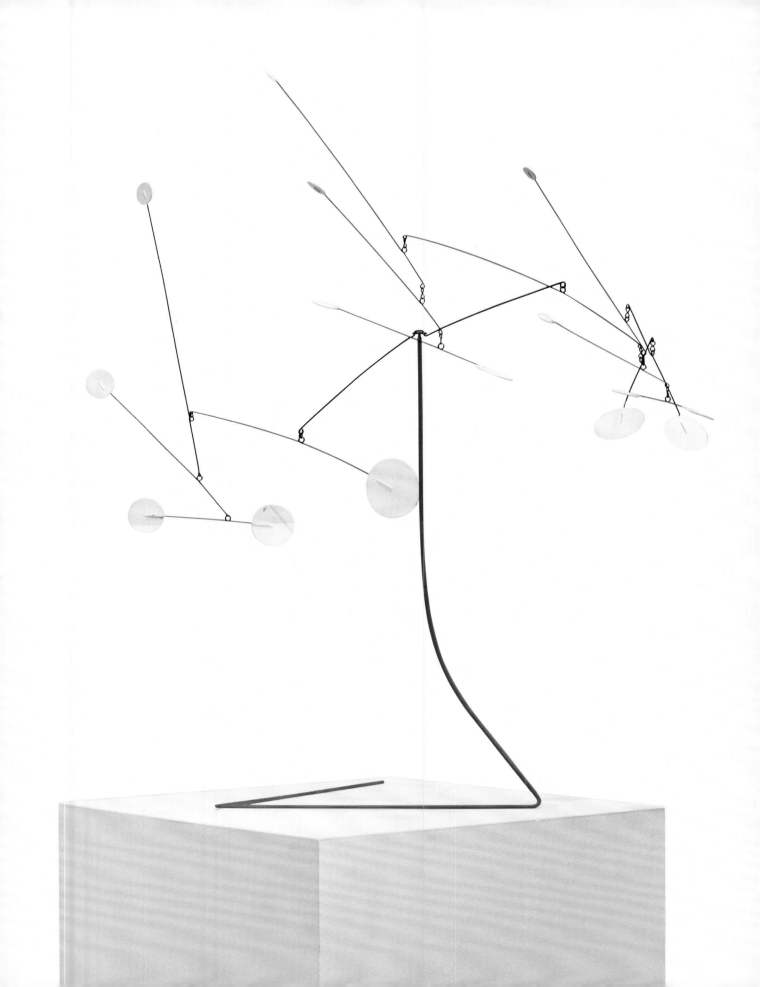

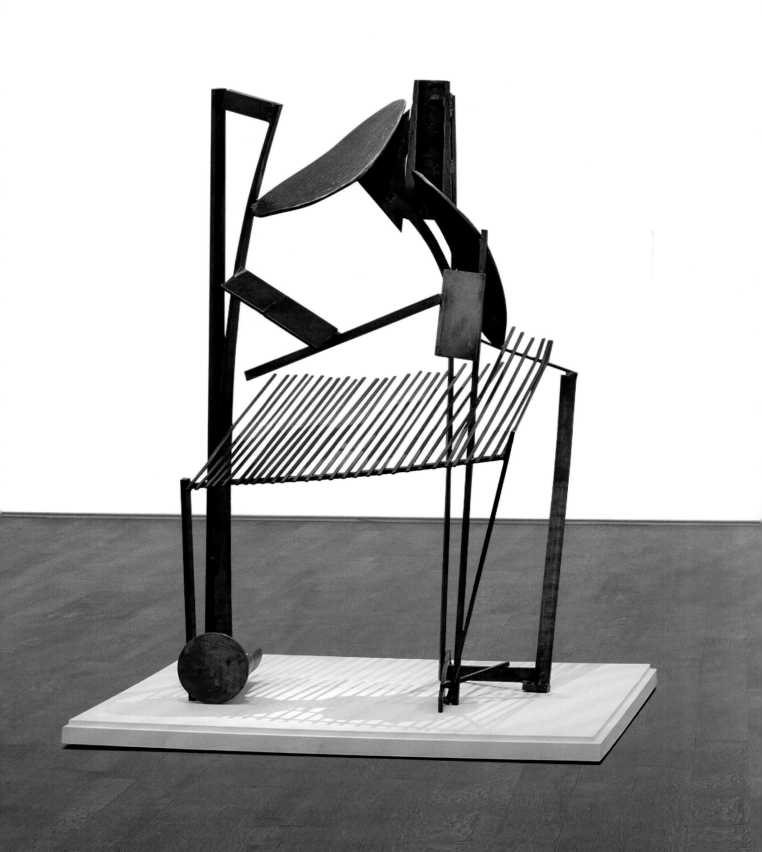

Anthony Caro

PLATE 7

Mint Chiffon

1979–80
Bronze
54 x 33 x 24 inches (137.2 x 83.8 x 61 cm)

Eduardo Chillida

PLATE 8

The Liberty Door I

1983
Steel
23 $\frac{1}{2}$ x 17 $\frac{1}{2}$ x 14 $\frac{1}{4}$ inches (59.7 x 44.5 x 36.2 cm)

Edgar Degas

PLATE 9

Dancer Looking at the Sole of Her Right Foot

1896–1911
Bronze, cast 69Q
19 $\frac{1}{4}$ x 13 $\frac{3}{16}$ x 8 $\frac{3}{16}$ inches (49 x 33.5 x 22.5 cm)

Lucio Fontana

PLATE 10

Concetto spaziale, Attese

1959
Waterpaint on canvas
28 $^1/_8$ x 31 $^1/_8$ inches (71.4 x 79.1 cm)

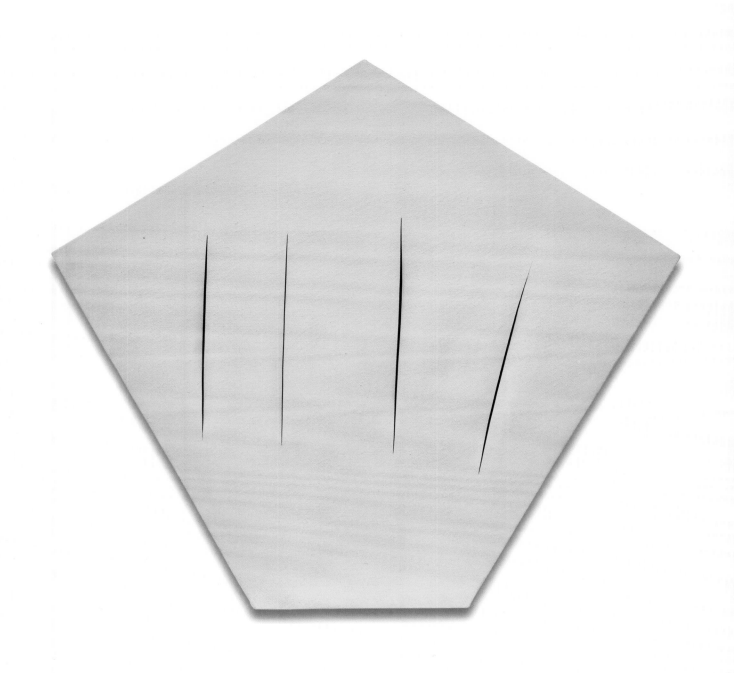

Eva Hesse

PLATE 11

Untitled (Bochner Compart)

1966
Acrylic and cord on papier-mâché and Masonite
9 x 9 x 2 inches (22.9 x 22.9 x 5.1 cm)

David Hockney

PLATE 12

Henry Reading

1985
Collage, acrylic, contact paper, charcoal on
gatorboard in artist's frame
92 $\frac{1}{2}$ x 57 $\frac{1}{2}$ inches (234.9 x 146.1 cm)

Mike Kelley

PLATE 13

*Empathy Displacement: Humanoid Morphology
(2nd and 3rd Remove) #8*

1990
Mixed-media construction comprising an acrylic painting on panel and
a found handmade doll, in a painted wood box
Panel: 46 $^3/_4$ x 21 inches (118.8 x 53.3 cm)
Box: 17 $^3/_4$ x 8 $^1/_2$ x 4 $^3/_4$ inches (45 x 21.6 x 12 cm)

Henri Laurens

PLATE 14

La Lune (*The Moon*)

1946
Bronze with brown and green patina, cast 2/4
35 $\frac{1}{2}$ x 19 x 35 $\frac{1}{2}$ inches (90.2 x 48.3 x 90.2 cm)

Fausto Melotti

PLATE 15

Senza titolo (Untitled)

c. 1946
Painted clay
22 $^7/_{16}$ x 26 $^3/_4$ x 2 $^9/_{16}$ inches (57 x 68 x 6.5 cm)

Joan Miró

PLATE 16

Le Voilier (The Sailboat)

1956
Earthenware
11$\frac{1}{2}$ x 9$\frac{7}{8}$ x 12 inches (29.2 x 25.1 x 30.5 cm)

Joan Miró

PLATE 17

Homme et femme dans la nuit (Man and Woman in the Night)

1969
Painted bronze, cast 1/4
34 $^1/_2$ x 16 $^1/_4$ x 16 inches (87.6 x 41.3 x 40.6 cm) and
29 x 16 $^5/_8$ x 17 $^1/_2$ inches (73.7 x 42.2 x 44.5 cm)

Henry Moore

PLATE 18

Reclining Figure No. 2

1953
Bronze with brown and green patina
36 inches long (91.4 cm)

Claes Oldenburg

PLATE 19

Soft Juicit—"Ghost" Version

1965
Canvas filled with kapok, burlap painted with Liquitex
on wood base covered with canvas
19 x 18 x 16 inches (48.3 x 45.7 x 40.6 cm)

Pablo Picasso

PLATE 20

Le Taureau (*The Bull*)

c. 1949–50
Varnished wood and plaster
26 $^{3}/_{4}$ inches long (68 cm)

Pablo Picasso

PLATE 21

Figures and Heads

1954
Red earthenware clay with engine and relief engraving, Edition 18/25
22 x 9 $\frac{3}{8}$ x 9 $\frac{3}{4}$ inches (55.9 x 23.8 x 24.8 cm)

James Rosenquist

PLATE 22

Untitled

1991
Heart-shaped box top covered in shirt fabric, tie,
plastic orchid and paper collage
10 x 9 $^1/_2$ inches (25.4 x 24.1 cm)

George Segal

PLATE 23

Cézanne Still Life #4

1981
Painted plaster, wood and metal
57 x 48 x 24 inches (144.8 x 121.9 x 61 cm)

Joaquín Torres-García

PLATE 24

Objet plastique (*Plastic Object*)

1929
Oil on wood
9 $^3/_4$ x 4 $^1/_4$ x 3 $^5/_{16}$ inches (24.8 x 10.8 x 8.4 cm)

Image Credits

PLATE 1: © El Anatsui
PLATES 2–4: © 2017 Miquel Barceló / Artists Rights Society (ARS), New York / ADAGP, Paris
PLATE 5: © The Easton Foundation / Licensed by VAGA, New York, NY
PLATE 6: © 2017 Calder Foundation, New York / Artists Rights Society (ARS), New York
PLATE 7: © Courtesy of Barford Sculptures Limited
PLATE 8: © Zabalaga-Leku, Artists Rights Society (ARS), New York 2017
PLATE 10: © 2017 Artists Rights Society (ARS), New York / SIAE, Rome
PLATE 11: © The Estate of Eva Hesse. Courtesy Hauser & Wirth.
PLATE 12: © David Hockney
PLATE 13: © Mike Kelley Foundation for the Arts. All Rights Reserved / Licensed by VAGA, New York, NY.
PLATE 14: © 2017 Artists Rights Society (ARS), New York / ADAGP, Paris
PLATE 15: © Fondazione Fausto Melotti. Courtesy the Estate of Fausto Melotti and Hauser & Wirth.
PLATES 16–17: © 2017 Successió Miró / Artists Rights Society (ARS), New York / ADAGP, Paris
PLATE 18: Reproduced by permission of The Henry Moore Foundation.
PLATE 19: Copyright 1965 Claes Oldenburg
PLATES 20–21: © 2017 Estate of Pablo Picasso / Artists Rights Society (ARS), New York
PLATE 22: © Estate of James Rosenquist / Licensed by VAGA, New York, NY
PLATE 23: © The George and Helen Segal Foundation / Licensed by VAGA, New York, NY
PLATE 24: © Alejandra, Aurelio and Claudio Torres, Sucesión J. Torres-García, Montevideo 2017

All photographs by Kent Pell.